D0330015

THE ACTOR

A Photographic Interview
with Ronald Reagan

GERALD GARDNER

PUBLISHED BY POCKET BOOKS NEW YORK

To Bob, Paul and Kal—
my peerless panel

 POCKET BOOKS, a Simon & Schuster division of
GULF & WESTERN CORPORATION
1230 Avenue of the Americas, New York, N.Y. 10020

ISBN: 0-671-43239-7

First Pocket Books printing April 1981

10 9 8 7 6 5 4 3 2 1

POCKET and colophon are trademarks of Simon & Schuster

Printed in the U.S.A.

Introduction

The wonderful thing about being an actor is that you can use your talent in so many ways. For example, the actor who is the subject of this book has used his talent to become the President of the United States.

Other actors are following his lead. They recently offered Robert De Niro the Governorship of Nevada, but he said he wouldn't be Governor unless they gave him script approval.

Now that we have an actor in the White House, many people are speculating on how well he will function in that post. There is a clue to the answer in his performance as Governor of the State of California...

In October 1969, an anguished woman appeared at the office of Governor Reagan in Sacramento. Her name was Harriet Cosgrove and she was seeking a stay of execution for her husband who was scheduled to die that night.

She was shown into the Governor's office by a neatly dressed aide. The woman observed a pile of movie scripts on the Governor's desk and posters from several vintage movies on the wall. But the Governor was nowhere in evidence.

"Will he be here soon?" she asked.

"Have a little patience, Mrs. Cosgrove. The Governor's a busy man," said the aide. "He's planting a tree on the south lawn."

"But there's no time!" cried the woman. "My husband will die in the gas chamber unless the Governor signs this Stay of Execution."

"Be patient. He'll finish with the tree any moment now."

Just then the office door opened and Governor Reagan entered, looking ruddy and smiling pleasantly.

"Morning, Paul," he said.

"Governor, Mrs. Cosgrove was anxious to see you—"

The woman cut in.

"Governor, in five minutes my husband will die—you must save him—you can't snuff out a human life—"

The Governor nodded solemnly, toying with a pencil, then stared intently at the sobbing woman.

"Did you see me in *Wings for the Eagle*?" he said.

"No," she said.

"Same situation. A man in the death house—I think it was Dennis Morgan. And Ida Lupino stood right where you're standing and begged for his life."

The woman rushed up to the Governor, faced him beseechingly. He moved her gently to one side.

"You're upstaging me," he said.

"Governor—my husband will *die*—"

"Same situation exactly," said the Governor. He turned to his aide. "What did I do in that picture? I think I let him fry."

The aide struggled to remember, then smiled.

"That picture is on the Late Show tonight, Governor."

"What time?"

"Eleven forty-five," said the aide.

"Won't help," said the Governor.

Reagan frowned resolutely.

"I'll tell you what—let's recreate the scene. That might bring it back. Mrs. Cosgrove, you stand right there—down-stage right."

"You don't understand," said the woman, "my husband is in the death house—"

"How did he get in a spot like that? Who's his agent?"

That triggered another torrent of tears.

"Governor, a human life will be extinguished unless you act!"

Reagan turned to his aide.

"We should have gotten Ida Lupino. She's trying to make it *her* scene."

"Governor, my husband—"

"Mrs. Cosgrove, I've given this matter a great deal of thought and I have reached a decision. I will grant this Stay of Execution." Reagan consulted his watch. "We don't have much time—"

"Less than thirty seconds," interrupted the woman.

"Don't step on my line," said the Governor.

Reagan sat down behind his desk, scrawled his signature on the document and handed it to the woman. She seized the Governor, kissed him emotionally, and hurried from the room.

For a long while the Governor sat staring after the retreating figure of the woman. Finally he frowned and turned to his aide.

"Paul, I think I may have made a terrible mistake...It wasn't Dennis Morgan in the death house. It was Sheldon Leonard...Ida Lupino played the warden."

**YOU HAVE SAID YOU MIGHT APPOINT A
WOMAN TO THE SUPREME COURT.
HOW WOULD YOU DECIDE WHICH
WOMAN TO PICK?**

YOU HAVE OPPOSED THE PROGRESSIVE INCOME TAX. DON'T YOU REALIZE THAT IF THE PROGRESSIVE INCOME TAX WERE ABOLISHED, THE RICH WOULD HAVE A GREAT ADVANTAGE OVER THE POOR?

YOU HAVE BEEN INTOLERANT OF OTHER SEXUAL LIFE STYLES, AND ESPECIALLY CRITICAL OF THE GAY COMMUNITY. BUT PERHAPS YOU ARE MERELY IGNORANT OF THEIR WAYS. FOR EXAMPLE, DO YOU KNOW HOW HOMOSEXUALS MAKE LOVE?

EVERYONE WOULD LIKE TO HAVE A POST WITH THE NEW ADMINISTRATION. WHO HAS BEEN THE MOST PERSISTENT JOB-SEEKER?

. . .

WHEN YOU WERE MAKING FILMS BACK IN THE FORTIES, THE HAYS OFFICE WAS VERY SCRUPULOUS ABOUT EVERYTHING FROM LANGUAGE TO THE WAY YOU KISSED THE HEROINE. HOW DID MOVIE STARS KISS BACK IN THE FORTIES?

YOU WILL BE MEETING WITH HEADS
OF STATE FROM COUNTRIES ALL OVER
THE WORLD. HOW WILL YOU BEGIN
THESE MEETINGS?

TO DISCOURAGE THEM FROM
PRACTICING SELF-ABUSE, SOME
PARENTS TELL THEIR CHILDREN THAT
MASTURBATION LEADS TO EVERYTHING
FROM INSANITY TO LOSS OF HEARING.
DO YOU FEEL THAT CHILDREN SHOULD
BE TOLD THESE OLD WIVES' TALES?

THE WHITE HOUSE COOK SAYS THAT EVERY MORNING, JUST BEFORE YOUR BREAKFAST, YOU HAVE SOMETHING COLD. WHAT IS IT?

YOU HAVE BEEN A MOVIE STAR, A GOVERNOR, AND NOW A PRESIDENT. IF YOU HAD YOUR WISH, WHAT ELSE WOULD YOU LIKE TO BE?

SOCIOLOGISTS SAY THAT 82 PERCENT
OF MARRIED MEN ARE UNFAITHFUL TO
THEIR WIVES AT LEAST ONCE.
HOW MANY TIMES HAVE YOU BEEN
UNFAITHFUL?

YOU FAVOR HARSH PENALTIES FOR SELLERS AND USERS OF HARD DRUGS, OWING TO THE DAMAGE THAT THESE DRUGS CAN CAUSE. HOW DID YOU LEARN OF THE DANGERS OF COCAINE?

YOUR MOST LOYAL ADVOCATE IS YOUR WIFE NANCY. SHE SAYS YOU HAVE ALL THE QUALITIES NECESSARY TO BE A TRULY GREAT PRESIDENT. WHAT DOES SHE FEEL IS THE BEST THING ABOUT YOU?

IN YOUR OPINION, WHICH WAY IS THE ECONOMY HEADED?

YOU HAVE DEPLORED THE SEXUAL PERMISSIVENESS OF OUR YOUTH. BUT AFTER ALL, SEX IS A NATURAL FUNCTION. YOUNG PEOPLE ARE DOING NO DIFFERENT THAN WHAT YOU DID ON YOUR HONEYMOON.

DESPITE REPORTS TO THE CONTRARY, YOUR WIFE IS A QUIET, PETITE WOMAN WITH A GENTLE LAUGH AND A DAINTY COUGH. WHAT IS HER SNEEZE LIKE?

EARLY IN THE CAMPAIGN, YOU QUESTIONED THE THEORY OF EVOLUTION, THEN BACKED AWAY FROM THIS VIEW. WHAT STARTED YOU THINKING THAT MAN MIGHT BE DESCENDED FROM THE APES?

NO ONE RECALLS EVER HEARING YOU UTTER AN OBSCENITY, EVEN A MILD ONE. WHAT DO YOU SAY WHEN YOU ARE ANGRY AT SOMEONE?

LAST OCTOBER JIMMY CARTER WAS THE MOST POWERFUL MAN IN THE UNITED STATES. TODAY HE IS LIVING IN A SHACK IN GEORGIA, REPUDIATED BY THE PUBLIC, ABANDONED BY HIS PARTY, DEFEATED, DEPRESSED AND DESTROYED.

MOST PRESIDENTS START TO DRAG AFTER A LONG DAY IN THE OVAL OFFICE. HOW DO YOU LOOK WHEN YOU FIRST START THE DAY?

YOUR DEBATE WITH JIMMY CARTER HAD A CRUCIAL EFFECT ON THE OUTCOME OF THE ELECTION. WHAT WAS THE MOST DIFFICULT PART OF THE DEBATE FOR YOU?

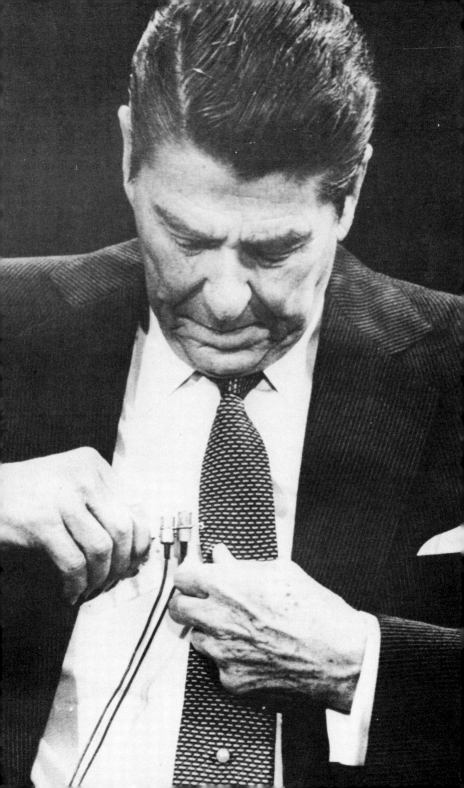

YOU HAVE PROMISED A LARGE ROLE FOR GEORGE BUSH. CAN YOU NAME ONE SPECIFIC THING HE'LL BE DOING?

GIVEN THE TREMENDOUS POWER OF NUCLEAR WEAPONS, YOUR MOST IMPORTANT TASK WILL BE TO PRESERVE THE PEACE. WHAT WILL YOU DO TO PREVENT A NUCLEAR WAR?

YOUR WIFE CAUSED YOU SOME EMBARRASSMENT WHEN SHE SUGGESTED THAT THE CARTERS LEAVE THE WHITE HOUSE EARLY SO SHE COULD REDECORATE. HOW DID YOU DEAL WITH THIS PROBLEM?

YOU ALMOST GOT YOUR BIG BREAK IN
FILMS IN 1937 WHEN YOU AND JOHNNY
WEISMULLER WERE BOTH UP FOR THE
SAME ROLE. WHAT DID YOU DO TO
AUDITION FOR THE ROLE OF TARZAN?

PRESIDENT KENNEDY ONCE SAW
4 AMBASSADORS, 12 CONGRESSMEN,
AND 15 AIDES BETWEEN 3:00 AND
5:00 P.M. AT THE WHITE HOUSE. WHAT
WOULD YOU BE DOING BETWEEN 3:00
AND 5:00 P.M.?

DURING THE INAUGURAL PARADE, SECRET SERVICE AGENTS SPOTTED A MAN WHO KEPT TRYING TO PUSH THROUGH THE CROWDS AND GET YOUR ATTENTION. WHO WAS HE?

WHEN YOU COULD NO LONGER GET MOVIE ROLES, YOU DECIDED TO TAKE A CRACK AT POLITICS. IF YOU HADN'T SUCCEEDED IN THAT, WHAT SORT OF WORK WOULD YOU HAVE DONE?

YOU HAVE OFTEN SEEMED INTOLERANT OF GAY RIGHTS. YET YOU MUST REALIZE THAT A LOT OF MEN PREFER TO MAKE LOVE TO OTHER MEN.

IT'S JUST A MINOR POINT IN THE TRANSITION—BUT WHAT DID YOU DO ABOUT AMY CARTER'S TREE HOUSE?

IN YOUR ACCEPTANCE SPEECH AT THE REPUBLICAN CONVENTION, YOU QUOTED FRANKLIN D. ROOSEVELT AND JOHN F. KENNEDY. YET THEY WERE BOTH DEMOCRATS.